# Computer Hacking

## A beginners guide to computer hacking, how to hack, internet skills, hacking techniques, and more!

# Table Of Contents

# Introduction

I want to thank you and congratulate you for downloading the book, "Computer Hacking".

This book contains helpful information about computer hacking, and the skills required to hack.

This book is aimed at beginners, and will take you through the basics of computer hacking. You will learn about the different types of hacking, the primary hacking methods, and different areas of a system that can be hacked.

This book includes great tips and techniques that will help you to begin developing your own computer hacking skills! You will discover some basic hacks you can do right away, and be pointed in the direction of software that will assist your hacking escapades.

However, keep in mind that hacking should be done in an ethical manner. White hat hacking is the only hacking you should be doing, so remember to keep your morals in check as your hacking skills improve!

Thanks again for downloading this book, I hope you enjoy it!

# Chapter 1:
# What is Hacking?

The term "hacker" today has garnered a negative connotation. You've heard about hackers breaking into computer systems and looking at or even stealing some very sensitive and very private information. Millions of computer users worldwide have felt the effects of hacking activity. That includes virus attacks, spyware, and other forms of malware that slow down, break into, or even cripple your computer system.

However, not all hackers are dubious and unscrupulous souls who have nothing better to do in life. In fact, the term "hacker" originally had a very positive and beneficial meaning to it. Traditionally, a hacker is someone who likes to tinker with computers and other forms of electronics. They enjoy figuring out how current systems work and find ways to improve them.

In other words, he used to be the guy who had to figure out how to make computers faster and better. Nowadays, a hacker is just someone who steals electronic information for their own self-interest. Nevertheless, there are still good hackers (white hat hackers) and bad hackers (black hat hackers).

It basically takes a hacker to catch a hacker and the good news is that a lot of them are on your side of the playing field. The premise of this book is to help you learn the basics of ethical hacking (the stuff that white hat hackers do). But in order to know what to look out for, you will have to catch a glimpse of what black hat hackers do.

The bottom line here is that hacking is no more than a set of computer skills that can be used for either good or bad. How one uses those skills will clearly define whether one is a white hat or a black hat hacker. The skills and tools are always neutral; only when they are used for malicious purposes do they take a turn for the worse.

## What are the Objectives of Ethical Hacking?

If hacking per se today is bent on stealing valuable information, ethical hacking on the other hand is used to identify possible weak points in your computer system or network and making them secure before the bad guys (aka the black hat hackers) use them against you. It's the objective of white hat hackers or ethical hackers to do security checks and keep everything secure.

That is also the reason why some professional white hat hackers are called penetration testing specialists. One rule of thumb to help distinguish penetration testing versus malicious hacking is that white hat hackers have the permission of the system's owner to try and break their security.

In the process, if the penetration testing is successful, the owner of the system will end up with a more secure computer system or network system. After all the penetration testing is completed, the ethical hacker, the one who's doing the legal hacking, will recommend security solutions and may even help implement them.

It is the goal of ethical hackers to hack into a system (the one where they were permitted and hired to hack, specifically by the system's owner) but they should do so in a non-destructive way. This means that even though they did hack into the system, they should not tamper with the system's operations.

Part of their goal is to discover as much vulnerability as they can. They should also be able to enumerate them and report back to the owner of the system that they hacked. It is also their job to prove each piece of vulnerability they discover. This may entail a demonstration or any other kind of evidence that they can present.

Ethical hackers often report to the owner of the system or at least to the part of a company's management that is responsible for system security. They work hand in hand with the company to keep the integrity of their computer systems and data. Their final goal is to have the results of their efforts implemented and make the system better secured.

## The Caveat

There is of course a caveat to all of this. For one thing, you can't expect to have all bases covered. The ideal of protecting any computer system or electronic system from all possible attacks is unrealistic. The only way you can do that is to unplug your system from the network and lock it away somewhere and keep it from all possible contact. By then the information contained in your system will remain useless to anyone.

No one, not even the best hacker in the world, can plan for everything. There are far too many unknowns in our highly connected world. John Chirillo even wrote an entire tome of possible hack attacks that can be performed on any number of systems. That's how many loopholes there are. However, you can test for all the best as well all the known possible attacks. If there is a new way of breaking in, then you can hire an ethical hacker to help you figure out a way to create a countermeasure. Using those means, you can tell that your systems are virtually safe for the time being. You just need to update your security from time to time.

# Chapter 2:
# Ethical Hacking 101

As part of ethical hacking, you should also know the actual dangers and vulnerabilities that your computer systems and networks face. Next time you connect your computer to the internet or host a WiFi connection for your friends, you ought to know that you are also opening a gateway (or gateways) for other people to break in.

In this chapter we'll look into some of the most common security vulnerabilities that ethical hackers will have to work with and eventually keep an eye on.

## Network Infrastructure Attacks

Network infrastructure attacks refer to hacks that break into local networks as well as on the Internet. A lot of networks can be accessed via the internet, which is why there are plenty out there that can be broken into. One way to hack into a network is to connect a modem to a local network. The modem should be connected to a computer that is behind the network's firewall.

Another method of breaking into a network is via NetBIOS, TCP/IP, and other transport mechanisms within a network. Some tricks include creating a denial of service by flooding the network with a huge load of requests.

Network analyzers capture data packets that travel across a network. The information they capture is then analyzed and the information in them is revealed. Another example of a fairly common network infrastructure hack is when people piggyback on WiFi networks that aren't secured. You may have heard of stories of some people who walk around the neighborhood with their laptops, tablets, or smartphones looking for an open WiFi signal coming from one of their neighbors.

## Non-Technical Attacks

Non-technical attacks basically involve manipulating people into divulging their passwords, willingly or not. The term social engineering comes to mind and it is the tool used in these kinds of attacks. An example of this is by duping (or even bribing) a coworker to divulge passwords and usernames. We'll look into social engineering a little later on.

Another form of non-technical attack is simply walking into another person's room where the computer is, booting the computer, and then gathering all the information that you need – yes it may sound like Tom Cruise and his mission impossible team, but in reality these non-technical attacks are a serious part of hacking tactics.

## Attacks on an Operating System

Operating system attacks are one of the more frequent hacks performed per quota. Well, it's simply a numbers game. There are many computers out there and a lot of them don't even have ample protection. There are a lot of loopholes in many operating systems – even the newest ones around still have a few bugs that can be exploited.

One of the avenues for operating system attacks is password hacking or hacking into encryption mechanisms. Some hackers are just obsessed with hacking other people's passwords just for the sheer thrill of it.

## Attacks on Applications

Apps, especially the ones online and the ones that deal with connectivity, get a lot of attacks. Examples of which include web applications and email server software applications. Some of the attacks include spam mail (remember the Love Bug or ILOVEYOU virus back in 2000?). Spam mail can carry pretty much anything that can hack into your computer system.

Malware or malicious software is also another tool in the hands of a hacker when they try to attack pretty much everything, especially apps. These software programs include Trojan horses, worms, viruses, and spyware. A lot of these programs can gain entry into your computer system online.

Another set of applications that get attacked frequently are SMTP applications (Simple Mail Transfer Protocols) and HTTP applications (Hypertext Transfer Protocols). Most of these applications are usually allowed to get by firewalls by the computer users themselves. They are allowed access simply because they are needed by the users or a company for its business operations.

## So Why Do You Have to Know All This?

You have to know the threat so you can perform it yourself and provide a way to protect a computer system from the said attack (or hack). Obviously, you can't beat an enemy you do not know. You can't counter a technique you don't know how to execute.

Note that this is only an introductory book, specifically designed for beginners. This book won't be able to cover all the hacking techniques out there. But at least you'll have an idea of how it's done and what tools you can use for your own systems testing.

**The Ethical Hacker Mindset**

Since this book will promote ethical hacking, you should become familiar with the white hat hacker's code and mindset. These involve some very basic rules of thumb that will help you along the way. They will also help you not to lose your way as you learn more technical hacking skills.

The first rule of thumb is to work ethically. You shouldn't have any hidden agendas, even when you have been given the thumbs up to hack into someone else's computer. Remember that you were hired to test for vulnerabilities in your employer's system. Needless to say, trust is a big tenet of ethical hackers.

The next rule of thumb is – don't crash the system. It doesn't matter if you're hacking into your own computer or if you're trying to break into someone else's computer system or network. Your goal is to find the loopholes but not to cause havoc. The system you hack should still be able to function as it should during and after you do your testing.

The last rule of thumb is to respect the other person's privacy. Even though you have the power to poke into someone else's private data, you're not supposed to interfere with their privacy. At the end of the day, you should be reporting any possible attacks on any form of private data.

# Chapter 3:
# Hacking Basics

In this chapter we'll look into some of the most basic hacking techniques and tools. These basic tools can be incorporated into other hacking techniques. Some of the tools and techniques that will be mentioned in this chapter aren't that technical. In fact, these may be the easiest of the many things you can learn in your white hat hacking career.

## Social Engineering

Social engineering is a non-technical hack. It doesn't mean that you have to go to Facebook or any other social media site just to gather someone else's information. It simply means taking advantage of the most commonly used resource available to computer users and companies as well – people. In the case of companies it's their employees.

By nature, people are trusting. It's natural to trust someone else, especially if you know the other person. This is one loophole that hackers try to take advantage of in any organization. All they need is a few details from one person, and then to use those details to gain more information from another employee and so on.

For instance they can pose as some kind of computer repair guy or a tech support representative and contact a customer of a certain company. They may talk the person into downloading some free software. The software was free but it wasn't what the hacker described it to be. The customer who trusted the service of said company downloads the files. The software that the customer downloaded then takes remote action without the customer's knowledge. Thus the hacker is able to gain valuable information.

They may claim to be this or that from a particular company to subscribers of a service. And at times they do not always ask a subscriber or customer to download something "free." They may even bluntly ask for the customer/subscriber's username and password. Since people are trusting, naturally, they divulge that information.

Phishing sites on the other hand do the same job. These websites are designed to gather login information. Some phishing sites even have some similar visual patterns or designs as the original site. Customers on Amazon may be tricked into signing into a phishing site that looks so much like Amazon. They login thinking the site is related to Amazon. The site then gathers the usernames and passwords of customers. Now, imagine if they could make people enter their credit card information, their PayPal logins, and other important bits of information!

Social engineering is one of the toughest hacks out there because you have to make yourself look official and legit to a complete stranger. However, once successful, it is also one of the hardest type of hack to counteract.

**Social Engineering Basic Steps**

The first step is to gather information about the company or people. Hackers can do the research themselves. They can use information filed with the SEC, finance organizations, and pretty much any other bit of useful information – there's a lot out there. The bigger the organization/company the more information there is you can find. Some hackers even pay someone else to look up all the information they need online.

Some hackers even check out the company's trash – yes they dumpster dive. Not a fond prospect but it turns up some very interesting documents at times. Some employees unwittingly throw away documents such as meeting notes, printed emails, organizational charts, network diagrams, a list of usernames/passwords, lists of internal phone numbers, and even their employee's handbook.

The next step is that they build trust. Hackers contact employees or customers using the information they have gained. They act as someone within the company. They often behave as a nice person – a person willing to help or in need of help. How believable they are depends on the amount of knowledge they have gathered. They don't always need to do face to face encounters or speak to their target in person. They can chat, send voice mail, or even send an email that looks official.

We have already mentioned the Love Bug as an example of this scenario. The creator of that worm virus also used social engineering to entice his targets to open the infected email. The email addresses of the targets came from email lists. When the target people saw the email they also saw that it came from one of their friends – so it was presumed safe to open. The virus program then gathered emails and other information from the target's computer and sends copies of itself in the form of other emails to other contacts.

Another fine example of social engineering is the Nigerian 419 scheme. Targets receive an email from someone they think they know and they offer to transfer a certain amount of money to their target's bank accounts. They ask for a little money to cover the transfer and the target's bank account information. Anyone who fell for it found out that their bank accounts no longer had funds the following day.

## Countermeasures to Social Engineering

The biggest countermeasure to social engineering is to inform the public. Keep your customers and employees aware of what official communication from the company looks like. People should become wary of anyone who asks for login information and other key bits of info.

## Compromising Physical Security Flaws

Physical security is actually a vital part of information security. Hackers can eventually find access to one of your computers. They can't get past your company's firewall but they can install a hardware or software within your network inside your firewall by simply walking in the door and connecting a device into one of your employee's computers.

Smaller companies that have few employees will have very little to worry about. These employees usually don't allow a stranger to use their computers. Larger companies have a bigger problem – they have more employees, more computer hardware, and plenty of other access points that hackers can use.

Hackers may not always want to just install a piece of hardware and have a point of entry from the inside. They may just need to access a computer, steal some important documents, or grab anything that seems to contain some vital information. They will usually have an alibi when asked. They will try to enter a building through any door including outside smoking areas where employees go to, cafeteria doors, fire escapes, or any entry point that is available. They may even just tailgate employees reentering a building and all they need to say to get in is "thank you for keeping the door open."

## Hacking Passwords

Hacking passwords is one of the hot activities for some hackers. However, note that it can be accomplished through social engineering and compromising physical vulnerabilities in the workplace. A simple way to hack someone else's password is to look over their shoulder as they enter it on a computer. Password hacking is one of the most common ways for hackers to access information via the network or a computer.

Another tactic is called inference. You gather as much information about an employee as you can (birthdates, names of children, their favorite stuff, important dates, phone numbers, favorite shows, and other stuff). Then you use those when you try to guess the password. You won't believe how many people just use the digits of their birthdates and other easy to remember numbers as passwords.

There are of course more high tech ways of guessing another person's password. The tools of the trade in terms of password hacking include network analyzers, remote cracking utilities, and other forms of password cracking software. You may also have heard about application programs that use "brute force." Brute force is a trial an error method of guessing the password. These programs try all possible combinations to try and guess the password. It may take quite a while before they can actually guess the password. This method is also called exhaustive key search.

Some hackers exploit physical flaws and try to gain access to another's computer just to locate passwords. Windows operating systems usually store passwords in the same directory or location known as the SAM or security accounts manager, for instance c:\...\win32\config directory or some other similar location. Sometimes passwords are stored in a database file that is still active like ntds.dit for instance. Some users create emergency repair disks or emergency repair files in a USB thumbdrive. All that's needed is access to the directory (e.g. c:\winnt\repair). Some passwords can also be found in the operating system's registry. And at times employees also save their passwords in a text file, which makes it easier for hackers.

Another way to crack another person's password especially if you have gained access to their computer is to install keyloggers. These are either pieces of software or hardware that log the keystrokes of unsuspecting users. Everything they type is recorded or logged. There are many keystroke logging software programs out there that can be bought or are given away for free. There are also hardware based keystroke-logging tools like a replacement keyboard or a keylogging tool that can be plugged into a USB port at the back of your target's computer.

# Chapter 4:
# Network Hacking

Network hacking is a practice that takes on many forms. One example is when people piggyback on another person's internet connection so they can surf the web for free. The other side of the coin is worse – now that you are inside a network you can scan the network and find some unsecured network device such as a computer or some other portable device that is connected to it. You can then try to access the information remotely.

One example of that is when you have logged into a WiFi network in a local café you can open your Windows explorer and click on Network. If file sharing and network discovery is turned on in that particular network then you can look for a connected computer or device and try to access the files contained in it. In this chapter we'll dive into the basics of network hacking.

## War Dialing

If you want to learn about the old school ways of hacking into another person's network then war dialing should satisfy your craving. This hacking method takes advantage of vulnerabilities in another person's telephone system. Yes, some people are still using dial up internet connections. Some network administrators even keep the old dial up connections as some sort of backup in case their main internet service goes down.

The tools of the trade in war dialing of course are war dialing software. Hackers can detect repeat dial tones. They can then enter a password at the dial tone and make calls anywhere –

for free. They can also access voice mail, especially for phone systems that use PBX switches.

## Network Structure Vulnerabilities

Computer networks have vulnerabilities. Even low level vulnerabilities can be avenues for hacking exploits. The very tools you use to hack networks are also the same tools that can be used to detect any vulnerability in your network.

You need network scanners that can perform trace routes, DNS lookups, and other network queries. Some scanners can also do port scanning and ping sweeps. There are those that can also do SMTP relay testing. You will also need a scanner that can do operating system fingerprinting and host port probing. There are network scanners that can also test firewalls.

Port scanners can tell you what devices are on your network. They're pretty easy to use and you can test any system with one. All of the commonly hacked ports make use of TCP protocols but some of them use UDP as well. The most common ports and the services associated with them include 23 (Telnet), 22 (SSH), 7 (Echo), 53 (DNS), 21 (FTP control), 80 (HTTP), 25 (SMTP), 443 (HTTPS), 19 (Chargen), 1433 (Microsoft SQL Server), and 20 (FTP data) among many others.

## Breaking Into WiFi Networks

Wireless networks that are run in the home, office, cafes, and pretty much anywhere are also avenues for hacking.

Back in the day, WiFi networks were kept open. That means if you had any device that could connect to the internet via a wireless connection, then all you needed to do was to search the area for some free open networks. Back then, when you bought a wireless router, the default configuration was open, which meant anyone could get on and piggyback on your internet.

Of course that caused a lot of problems. The more devices that are connected to your wireless connection the slower the service goes. Back in the day the only thing keeping hackers off your connection was the range of the signal coming from your WiFi router.

The common tools of the trade back then included directional antennas and signal amplifiers. Some of the more expensive tools can fish out your WiFi signal from miles away.

Back in the day, the only security available to WiFi router owners was WEP (Wireless Encryption Protocol). It worked for a time but it was poorly designed. Anyone can monitor your router's communication and eventually crack the WEP code.

Nowadays, users don't set limits to their WiFi signals, which is a good thing since you won't need to buy those crazy antennas. Most routers have a range of 1,500 feet nowadays (about 500 meters). The only different thing they're doing today is that the newer routers use WPA (WiFi Protected Access) and WPA2 (WiFi Protected Access 2) as their type of security protocols.

Theoretically, these new security protocols are much better than WEP – and they are. The old monitoring and WiFi cracking software tools will now take several days or even months to crack those codes. However, with the improvement in today's wireless security protocols, come improvements in the way wireless networks are hacked.

Nowadays, if you want to hack into your neighbor's wireless connection, you should monitor the wireless activity and catch the data (i.e. pocket capture) as their computer or any other authorized device is logging into the router or access point. Now, that may seem like a hard thing to come by given the fact that most people just keep their computers connected to their routers almost 24/7.

The good news is that there is a workaround this tough hurdle. All you need is to send out a deauth frame. What is that? Those are packets that you send to the access point (e.g. the wireless router) that de-authorizes other devices that are already connected to the network. Simply put, send those packets and all connected devices will be forced to login again. Since those devices will have to login again you have a chance to capture the login information.

**Tools for Hacking Into Wireless Connections**

The tools for hacking into wireless connections are available today. You will have to pay for the really good ones but there are open source (i.e. free) ones out there that will also do a decent job. You will have to look up and download what is known as penetration testing software (e.g. Aircrack-ng among many others). Some of these programs will cost you hundreds if not thousands of dollars. If that isn't a price you're comfortable with then you can just go with open source variants. They work too but they have their limits.

Wireless penetration testing programs can send deauth frames. After that they will capture pcap files for you (pcap = packet capture). Capturing the pcaps will take an hour or so. The next question is what do you do with the pcap files? Some penetration testing software can examine the data for you. However, if the functionality of your hacking tool is limited (since it's free) then you will have to get another tool to crack the pcap files – they're called password crackers.

Again, some password crackers are free and others are paid. Some of them you have to install onto your computer while others are online applications. The basic operation of these password crackers is that they check the pcap files against a database consisting of millions of possible passwords. Sometimes it only takes seconds before these software programs can crack the passwords.

One secret is that many routers nowadays still have WiFi Protected Setup enabled. Cracking software will usually break down the PIN into a couple of equal halves. The pin actually has 8 characters. Note that the last character of that pin is nothing more than a checksum. This means that the only digits/characters that need to be cracked are the first seven.

You may have encountered routers that do not broadcast its SSID, the name assigned by the user to the wireless network. You can figure it out using a war driving stumbler program. Some routers also have MAC filtering, which only allows listed devices to access the wireless network. That may also sound secure, however, MAC addresses on this list can also be captured in the same way that pcap files are captured. You can then copy or use the captured MAC addresses as your own, which is called spoofing. Yes, there are software tools that can spoof MAC addresses for you or you can do that by yourself by editing the registry.

# Chapter 5:
# Hacking Your Own Windows Password

Some people forget passwords – it happens every day. So what do you do when you or someone else you know gets locked out of their own computer? That's basically when your own trusty hacking skills (no matter how basic they might be) will come into play. However, you should remember that breaking into someone else's computer is considered illegal – unless they hired you to do it.

## Default Administrator Account

So, let's say that you have a machine that still runs Windows 7 (some people just hate Windows 8). One of the hacks that you can do is to use the Windows 7 Administrator account – the default one, yes. It's usually disabled when you boot the computer in normal mode. So, what you need to do is to boot the computer in Safe Mode.

Once the computer boots to Safe Mode, you must select the default administrator on Windows 7. It's the one that has no password requirement. You just leave the password box blank to log in. Once you're logged in you can go to Control Panel and change the password of the user account in question.

## Password Reset Disk

A password reset disk contains a small wizard program that will guide users to creating a new password for the locked Windows user account. This disk (or the password reset file, which can also be stored in a USB thumb drive) should have been created when the operating system was newly installed. Most people just make the reset disk and forget about it. Now that they have forgotten their Windows password, it's high time you help them remember where they put it. Once you have it, plug it into the computer and click "Reset Password."

All you need to do after that is to follow the prompts. You'll be asked where the password reset files are located, so select the proper drive where the file is located (i.e. the thumb drive). You will also be prompted to enter a new password. All you have to do after that is to follow the instructions that come up on the screen.

# Conclusion

Thank you again for downloading this book!

I hope this book was able to help you learn more about computer hacking!

The next step is to put the strategies provided into use, and begin learning to hack computers!

Finally, if you enjoyed this book, please take the time to share your thoughts and post a review on Amazon. It'd be greatly appreciated!

Thank you and good luck!

www.ingramcontent.com/pod-product-compliance
Lightning Source LLC
Chambersburg PA
CBHW071555080326
40690CB00056B/2048